ADAM AVOCADO

Illustrations by Angela Mitson Written by Giles Reed

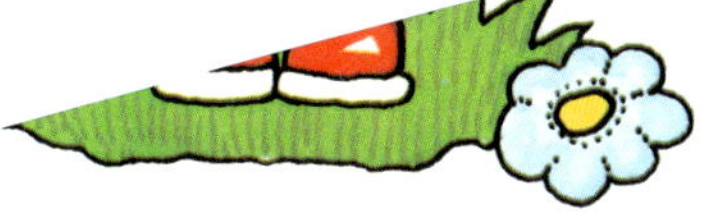

PUBLISHED BY STUDIO PUBLICATIONS (IPSWICH) LIMITED
32 PRINCES STREET, IPSWICH, SUFFOLK, ENGLAND.

Adam Avocado is one of the Munch Bunch.

He lives in a lantern next door to Pippa Pear.

Adam likes the girls. And all the girls like Adam.

Adam also likes cooking. And that morning he cooked a big fish for his breakfast.

He felt very happy, because this evening Lucy Lemon was coming to tea, and he was going to cook her a real Chinese meal.

When he'd finished his breakfast, and washed all the dishes, Adam went out for a walk.

Soon, he met Suzie Celery.

Now, Adam and Suzie are not very good friends. They are always playing tricks on each other.

"Good morning, Suzie," said Adam politely.

"Hello, Adam," she replied. "Are you coming to the dance in the Village Hall tonight?"

"Oh no," said Adam. "Lucy's coming to tea. And I'm cooking her a Chinese meal."

"Do you like my flower?" asked Adam with a grin. "It smells lovely."

Suzie didn't realise it was a trick flower. So she bent to smell it.

And Adam squirted water all over her.

Suzie Celery was furious!

She went to tell Pippa Pear what had happened.

Pippa was busy eating, as usual. And, when she heard the news, she was very cross, too.

"The rascal! He promised to take me to the dance tonight," she said. "Listen, Suzie, I've got a plan. We'll teach him a lesson. Chinese meal indeed!"

Adam had been busy in the kitchen all day, preparing the Chinese meal.

And, when Pippa and Suzie peeped through the window, the meal was almost ready.

Adam suddenly remembered something important. "I've forgotten to get Lucy some flowers," he said to himself. And he hurried out to get them.

Pippa and Suzie couldn't believe their luck!

As soon as he went out, they crept in and made a few changes to the Chinese food which Adam had so carefully prepared.

Then, they went back to the window to watch, and wait for the fun to start.

Soon, Adam returned with Lucy Lemon.

"This is ever so exciting," said Lucy. "I've never had a Chinese meal before."

"The first course is my speciality," said Adam. "It's called 'Bird's Nest Soup'."

Outside, Pippa and Suzie giggled. Their plan was about to start working.

Just as Adam and Lucy were about to start their soup, they heard a loud TWEET TWEET.

And suddenly, some very angry, wet birds flew into the air! Lucy was very surprised.

Pippa and Suzie thought their plan had got off to a good start.

The next course was Adam's favourite. It was Chop Suey.

But, all of a sudden, Lucy screamed . . . a real, live worm was wriggling along her chopstick, and smiling at her!

"I think we'd better leave this and start on the ice-cream," said poor Adam.

Pippa and Suzie couldn't wait to see the next part of their plan in action.

Just as Adam was bringing the ice-creams to the table, they gave one very big puff, and blew all the candles out.

And Lucy screamed again as a great big, hairy spider slowly appeared in front of her.

It was only a trick spider, but it took Adam a long time to calm Lucy down.

Surely, nothing could go wrong with the ice-cream?

But Suzie knew better. She had mixed some soap in the ice-cream which made it very bubbly.

In front of them all, the ice-cream started to spill out of the glasses. And it gradually crept across the table.

Adam cleared up the mess and then he went to get the coffee.

But, when he started to pour it, he found that the coffee-pot had suddenly developed a lot of leaks. And, as he poured a cup for Lucy, coffee showered all over the place.

Poor Adam was very unhappy.

He'd spent all day getting the meal ready. And it had all gone wrong.

And it was all too much for Lucy. She burst into tears. "Are all Chinese meals like this?" she sobbed.

"Oh no," said Adam. "And just to prove it, I'll take you to the Chinese Restaurant in the town. We'll have a proper Chinese meal cooked by Chinese men."

Pippa and Suzie were listening at the window.

"I've always wanted to go to that Chinese Restaurant," said Pippa. "I wish he was taking me."

"Me too," said Suzie.

That night, Adam and Lucy had the best Chinese meal they had ever eaten.

A.M.

And if Pippa and Suzie want to be taken to the Chinese Restaurant, they will just have to be nice to Adam in the future.

Won't they?